HIDDEN SPIRITS

SEARCH-AND-FIND SCENES FROM THE AMERICAN WEST

ART BY JUDY LARSON
TEXT BY SUE KASSIRER

RANDOM HOUSE NEW YORK

LAKE COUNTY PUBLIC LIBRARY

3 3113 01523 1782

For my children, Erik, Krister, and Rakel,
who inspire me daily to look beyond the obvious—J. L.

For Judy and Karen—S. K.

Our thanks to Dr. David Hurst Thomas, Curator of Anthropology
at the American Museum of Natural History, New York City,
for his expertise and enthusiasm

Text copyright © 1996 by Random House, Inc.
Illustrations copyright © 1996 by Judy Larson
All rights reserved under International and Pan-American Copyright
Conventions. Published in the United States by Random House, Inc.,
New York, and simultaneously in Canada by Random House of Canada
Limited, Toronto.

Judy Larson is represented exclusively by Applejack Limited Editions.

Library of Congress Cataloging in Publication Data
Larson, Judy L.
Hidden spirits : search-and-find scenes from the American
West / art by Judy Larson : text by Sue Kassirer.
    p.   cm.
ISBN 0-679-85803-2
1. Indians of North America—West, New—Juvenile literature. 2.
Mammals—West, New—Juvenile literature.   3. Birds—West, New—
Juvenile literature. [1. Indians of North America—West, New. 2.
West, New—Zoology. 3. Picture puzzles.] I. Kassirer, Sue. II. Title.
E78.S7L29   1996
398.24'590979—dc20
94-43395

Manufactured in the United States of America   10 9 8 7 6 5 4 3 2 1

Enter a world where the unseen is suddenly seen—where a simple rock may not be a rock at all but an eagle; where the bark on a tree reveals itself to be a wolf's eye; where eight ponies that seem to be traveling alone are found accompanied by two stampeding buffalo.

Enter the mysterious world of Judy Larson's American West—a world inspired by the wonders of nature and by the Native American belief in the life of the spirit.

Search for the hidden images and learn something about the American Indians and the wildlife of the area. Maybe you, like others before, will even find something—a bird, an animal, or a person—that the artist has never seen! You'll find answers at the back of the book.

PHANTOM PATROL

Nine pinto ponies enjoy their solitude. Over steep and snow-covered terrain, they gallop into a forest of spruce and birch. But are the ponies really alone? Find three more ponies and their riders.

The small size and shaggy coat of the pinto pony do not suggest speed and readiness. But these ponies, bred by Native Americans, were easily the match of European horses in battle or on the hunt.

American Indians prized and respected the horse, which was first introduced to them by the Spaniards in the early 1600s. Horses were large enough to carry heavy loads, and so replaced the much-loved dog as porters. Plains Indians gave their horses names such as Spirit Dog, Holy Dog, or Medicine Dog. One tribe, the Jicarilla Apache, considered horses to be gifts from supernatural powers.

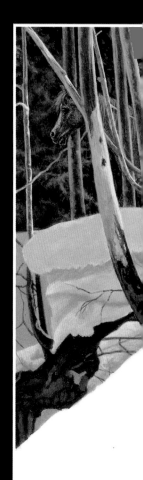

JudyLa

FOUR WOLVES

Three wolves emerge from beneath an overhang in the red sands of the desert and cause five wild pinto ponies to panic. The ponies run for their lives. But a fourth wolf runs with them. Or is it just the spirit of that wolf that won't let go? Find the one hidden wolf.

Wild horses still roam the American West today, thanks to the ongoing efforts of dedicated conservationists and horse lovers. But gone are the days when large herds of these majestic animals inhabited the area. The red and white of these ponies' coats serves as a good camouflage against the red sands and bright sunlight of the desert.

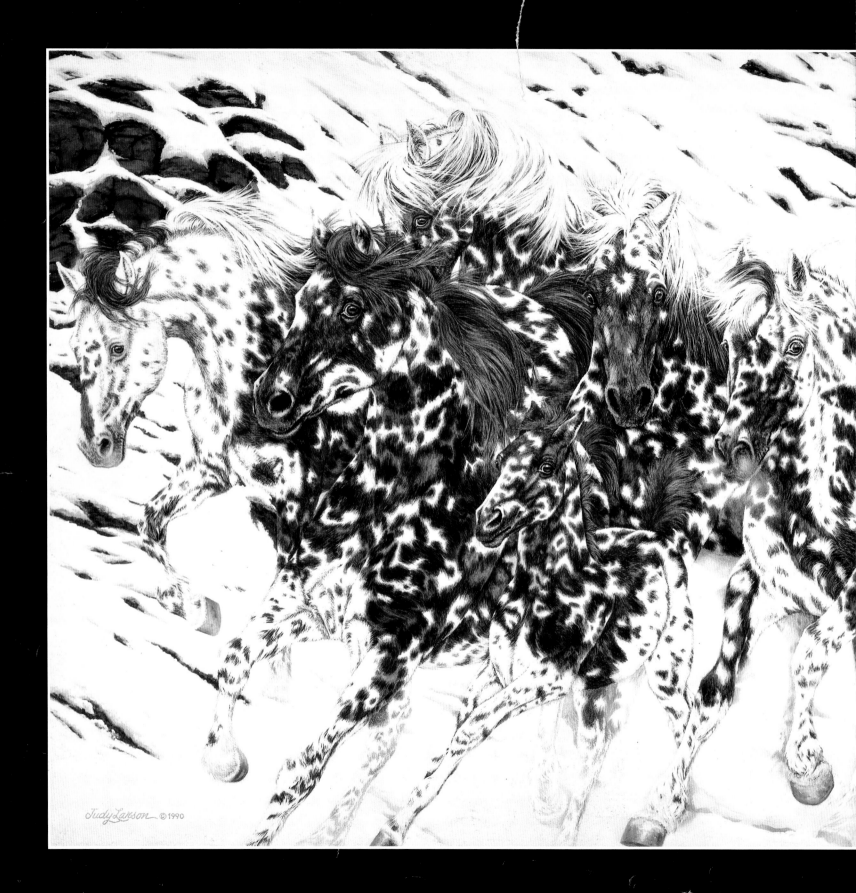

Judy Larson ©1990

MIXED COMPANY

Eight Appaloosas race closely together through the snow. They sense that they are not alone but in "mixed company." Find the two stampeding buffalo.

Because the coats of these spotted ponies looked like natural warpaint, many Native Americans felt that they had been specially chosen by the spirits for battle or the hunt. In fact, the Nez Perce Indians of the Plains were so impressed by these ponies that they began to breed them—and became America's first horse breeders. They named them Appaloosa after the Palouse River, which ran through their homeland.

Judy Larson ©1991

CROW PONIES

Two Appaloosas suddenly pull up short. They hear a fluttering of crows' wings, but no birds appear. Why can't they see the birds? Find the three crows that make these Appaloosas "Crow ponies" in more ways than one.

The red and blue paint distinguishes these ponies as belonging to the Crow Indian tribe, and earns them their "Crow pony" nickname. The Crow Indians migrated to the northern Great Plains at least 300 years ago and still inhabit the area. They call themselves *Apsaalooke*, which means "children of the large-beaked bird."

Indeed, crows' beaks are not only large but strong and sharply pointed as well. When crows see a predator, they call one another with repeated long, loud cries. Then they gather together and drive the predator away with their beaks.

WHEREWOLVES

Two red foxes take a quiet walk in the woods. But when they spot some days-old wolf tracks melting in the patchy snow, they sense danger. Is that the sound of a branch cracking underfoot? Is that an eye peering out? And what about that ancient Indian carving on a rock? Nine wolves silently close in around the wary foxes. But they look frozen in time—except for one, lurking in the distance… Find the nine hidden wolves.

Thousands of wolves once roamed and hunted in packs in the American Southwest. Today the wolf has, sadly, become nearly extinct worldwide because of hunting, trapping, poisoning, and changes that humans have made in the environment. But there is hope for the wolves. They have recently been reintroduced into Yellowstone National Park in Wyoming, and perhaps they will flourish once again. In the meantime, the spirit of the wolves lives on.

FOWL PLAY

A playful coyote leaps into action as a golden eagle feather drifts to the ground. But hidden in the silent rocks are nine other eagle feathers, which tell of brave deeds of war in battles long ago. Find the nine eagle feathers.

Golden eagle feathers were awarded to Plains Indian warriors for "counting coup," which meant touching a live enemy with a hand-held object. In order to achieve manhood, one needed to earn a certain quota of coup. Killing an enemy did not earn one the most coup. Rather, one was more highly rewarded for having had the chance to kill someone and for not having done so.

The feathers were notched, clipped, dyed, or otherwise altered to symbolize specific skillful and courageous acts.

warrior's first coup

warrior counted coup four times

warrior counted coup five times

warrior killed enemy

warrior cut enemy's throat

warrior cut enemy's throat and took his scalp

warrior was wounded

warrior was wounded many times

warrior was wounded, but still killed enemies (one quillwork band per kill)

SEEN BUT NOT HEARD

Two wolves are stopped short by something moving in the distance. They spin around, but it's gone. Or was it never there in the first place? Find the Native American on horseback about to overcome the buffalo.

At one time, as many as 60 million buffalo roamed the Plains region. Buffalo meat and hides were basic to the lives of many American Indians. In fact, the Plains Indians used every part of the buffalo, with no waste whatsoever.

Once horses were introduced by Europeans, hunting the buffalo became an easier task. But a buffalo could seriously injure or even kill a horse.

Judy Larson

MAKING TRACKS

The rocks and trees reveal the presence of a mountain lion who has "made tracks"—but in spirit only. Yet the Apache and his pony instinctively sense the existence of a real mountain lion and will, in an instant, be making tracks of their own. Find the one hidden mountain lion and three paw prints.

Mountain lions have lived in the Southwest for centuries and still make their homes there. The Apache Indians felt that the mountain lion had special powers, and so offered its meat to shamans, or holy men, only.

Horses can sense the presence of a mountain lion before they see one, and an experienced rider will be tipped off by the way the horse tosses its mane.

Judy Larson ©1989

BEARLY SEEN

A grizzly takes a cool dip on a hot summer's day. But what are those slight movements in the boulders beyond his bathing pool? Two figures dart in and out of view. Has the grizzly seen them? Will they escape in time? The next few moments will decide their fate. Find the two hidden Apache Indians.

Although they have been extinct in the Southwest for decades, grizzlies were once very much at home in this area. Awesome creatures, they have been known to weigh as much as 1,000 pounds and stand eight feet tall. It's no wonder that they are the subject of dozens of North American Indian legends.

Judy Larson 231/1500   Judy Larson ©

GONE WITH THE WIND

An Appaloosa making his way through a rocky area is caught off guard by the sight of a soaring eagle. But does he know that there are really three eagles close by? Find the other two.

Symbolizing sacred power to many Native Americans, eagles were the most honored of all birds. There was a time when many eagles nested on the red rocky cliffs of the Southwest. But now, with pesticides weakening their eggs and poachers hunting them, only a few nesting pairs remain. What once was is now gone forever.

ABOUT THE ART

Judy Larson used a method called *scratchboard* to make the art in this book. Scratchboard is an artistic technique that requires a great deal of patience.

Before she even lifts a tool, Ms. Larson spends a long time thinking about and planning each painting. After she has a picture clearly in mind, she makes a rough sketch. The sketch always includes the camouflaged images. They are never added later in the process.

Once the sketch is done, Ms. Larson begins working on a thin board coated with a layer of hardened white china clay (*see Figure 1, facing page*). The board is called a scratchboard, just like the artistic technique.

First she paints in her main subject (usually an animal) with permanent black india ink (*see Figure 2*). When the ink is dry, she uses white chalk to trace an outline on the black image.

She next uses a tool called an X-Acto knife to scratch away the black ink wherever she needs to make a line. This reveals the white china clay underneath (*Figure 3*). Once she has finished scratching away the black ink, she is left with a finely detailed black-and-white image (*Figure 4*). She sometimes uses up to one hundred blades to scratch out a single painting!

Color is added with transparent permanent inks. These are applied with an airbrush, a tool that sprays a fine mist of paint. Certain areas are then rescratched and airbrushed a second time. Finishing touches are painted with gouache or acrylics, which are both water-based paints.

Ms. Larson paints her backgrounds (including the hidden images) with acrylics or gouache. It is necessary to use many coats, because the white clay of the scratchboard soaks up paint like a sponge.

If you look back at the artwork in this book, you should now be able to tell which parts were "scratched" and which were painted with gouache or acrylics. You can see the very fine lines and detail in the scratchboard art.

Scratchboard kits can be found in most art supply and arts and crafts stores.

Figure 1 Smooth white scratchboard

Figure 2 Subject inked

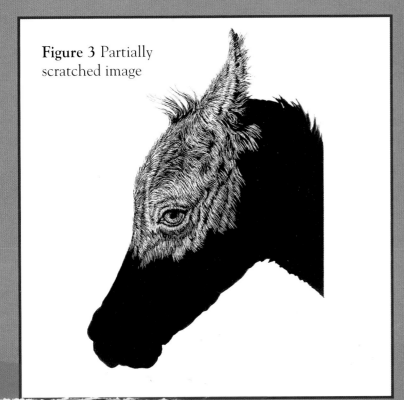

Figure 3 Partially scratched image

Figure 4 Finished image

Phantom Patrol

Four Wolves

Mixed Company

Crow Ponies

real wolf

Wherewolves

Fowl Play

Seen but Not Heard

Making Tracks

Bearly Seen

Gone with the Wind

Judy Larson has seen and thought about hidden images from as far back as childhood. She recalls how she used to look up from her bed in the morning and see wondrous shapes of animals and people in the play of light on her stucco ceiling. At night she would lie under the covers and draw the images by flashlight.

Indeed, Ms. Larson knew, even as a young child, that she would be an artist someday. She was born in Southern California into a family of professional artists, and it was her father, more than anyone, who inspired her to take the same route. She received her Bachelor of Science degree in commercial art from Pacific Union College, in Northern California, then spent the next seventeen years working as a commercial artist, illustrator, and art director both in the Midwest and on the West Coast.

Since 1973 Ms. Larson has worked out of her home, where she lives with her three children, four dogs, three cats, numerous fish, and one hermit crab—not to mention two horses out back. A true nature lover, Ms. Larson now devotes her talents to wildlife art. The main focus of each work is always the animal, with images often hidden in the landscape as reminders of the uniqueness and beauty of Native American culture.

Ms. Larson uses scratchboard as her medium (*see "About the Art"*). A member of numerous wildlife and conservation organizations and humane societies, she has received many awards for her works, which can be found in private collections from Australia to Saudi Arabia and as far north as the Bering Strait. "Wherewolves" was honored as one of the best-selling prints of 1990 by *U.S. Art* magazine. Her prints are sold by galleries throughout the United States, Canada, and Great Britain, and are published exclusively by Applejack Limited Editions of Manchester Center, Vermont.

Sue Kassirer is a children's book editor and writer who developed the idea for *Hidden Spirits* after coming across a print of "Wherewolves" at a crafts fair one summer in Connecticut. Struck by the extraordinary playfulness yet uncompromising quality of Judy Larson's art, she purchased the print, thinking that children would delight in its hidden images as well as its Western theme.

But when Ms. Kassirer attempted to contact Ms. Larson about a book project, she ran into trouble. Who *was* Judy Larson? Where did she live? Would she want to work on a book for children? The dealer at the crafts fair had supplied little information. And so, armed only with a name, Ms. Kassirer embarked on a search that turned out to be fitting, for it was not unlike the search for the artist's hidden images. Judy Larson remained elusive.

Finally, after months of unsuccessful sleuthing, Ms. Kassirer was thrilled to discover, in the stacks of the New York Public Library, a magazine of Southwest wildlife art. It contained a full-page ad for limited-edition prints of Ms. Larson's works—and, most important, the name of her art publisher.

But the search was not yet over—numerous phone calls and letters to the publisher went unanswered. It was only in February of the following year that Ms. Kassirer finally tracked down Ms. Larson's current art publisher. Within days, Judy Larson contacted Ms. Kassirer. The two women hit it off and, working on opposite coasts, produced *Hidden Spirits*.

Ms. Kassirer studied fine arts at Bard College and received a Bachelor of Arts degree in English literature from the State University of New York College at Purchase. She lives in New York City with her husband, Tom, and daughter, Laura.

JUV P LARS   DS
Larson, Judy L.
Hidden spirits

5-15-96

⟨7⟩

Ex-Library: Friends of
Lake County Public Library

LAKE COUNTY PUBLIC LIBRARY
INDIANA

AD	FF	MU
AV	GR	NC
BO	HI	SJ
CL	HO	CN L
DS MAY 1 1 1996	LS	

THIS BOOK IS RENEWABLE BY PHONE OR IN PERSON IF THERE IS NO RESERVE
WAITING OR FINE DUE.

LCP #0390